From Verdun
Bibliothèque Municipale MS. 107 Breviary, Part II, for
Marguerite de Bar, Verdun use, Lorraine, about 1300

The margins of medieval manuscripts were often filled with small pictures of people, animals and fantastic creatures. Several pictures in this book were taken from such marginal figures; a few do not have names.

From the Echternach Gospels, Northumbrian,
c. 690 A.D., Paris, Bibliothèque Nationale,
Lat. 9389. Cat. 395

THE ECHTERNACH LION

of Modena. Early 13th Century. Inscribed
ARTUS DE BRETANIA.

THE EARLIEST PICTURE OF KING ARTHUR

King Arthur is thought to have lived in Cornwall early in the Sixth Century.   He led the Britons in battle against the Saxon invaders.

From an ivory plaque,
Florence, Museo Nazionale
del Bargello, 9th–10th century

A BYZANTINE WARRIOR

Constantinople was the capital of the Byzantine Empire, which was founded by Constantine as the eastern part of the Roman Empire.
The Byzantine Empire survived for many centuries after the decline of Rome, but it was finally conquered by the Turks in 1453.

SAINT GEORGE AND THE DRAGON

A MONK COPYING A BOOK

Books were written by hand, usually on sheepskin instead of paper. The pen was made of a sharpened
feather, and a knife was used to scrape away mistakes.

BIRDS AND BEASTS

CHARLEMAGNE, which means Charles the Great,
was king of the Franks. He conquered a large part of Europe and on
Christmas Day in 800 he was crowned Emperor of the West.

From Chronique de l'Anonyme de Bethune,
Paris, Bibliothèque Nationale, nouv. acq.
fr. 6295, f. 29; 2nd half of the 13th century.

ROLAND BLOWING HIS HORN

Roland was the leader of the rear-guard in Charlemagne's army, which fought the Saracens at Roncevaux, in the Pyrenees, in 778. When he knew that his men were losing, Roland blew his horn to warn Charlemagne, who was 30 leagues away.

From an inscribed stone, Stenkyrka,
Visbi, Gotland's Fornsal
about 800 A.D.

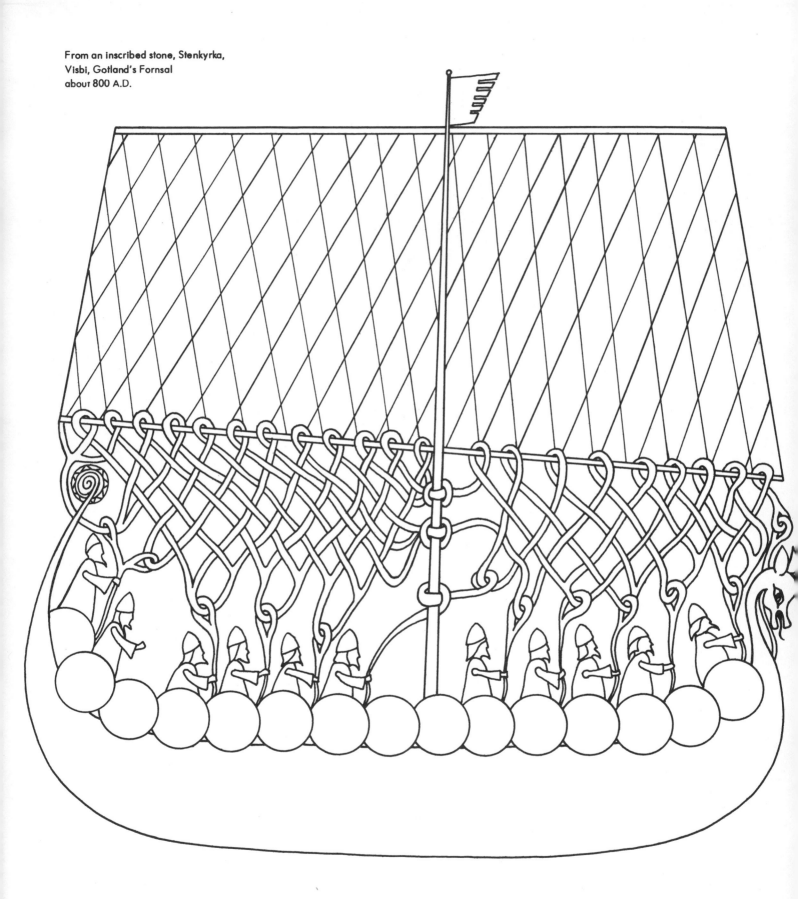

A VIKING SHIP

From the Bayeux Tapestry

WILLIAM THE CONQUEROR
1066

William, Duke of Normandy, was offered the succession to the throne of England by King Edward the Confessor, and Earl Harold of Wessex had promised to support Duke William. Upon the death of King Edward, however, Harold changed his mind, and took the crown himself. Hearing this, Duke William prepared his army and sailed to England, where, at Hastings, in 1066, near a grey apple tree, the Normans defeated Harold and his English army. William was crowned King of England on Christmas Day, 1066.

THE NORMANS CROSSING THE CHANNEL TO INVADE ENGLAND
1066

From the Bayeux Tapestry

A LADY WITH A FALCON
Hunting with falcons was a favorite sport in the Middle Ages.

From Verdun. Bibliothèque Municipale MS. 107. Breviary of Marguerite de Bar, f. 12, Lorraine, about 1300.

KING ARTHUR ON HIS THRONE

WITH THE THREE CROWNS OF ENGLAND, SCOTLAND, AND BRITTANY

From the seal of Duke Conrad of Masovia
Poland, 1238

A CRUSADER

The Crusades were expeditions to free the Holy Land from the Moslems. The First Crusade set out in 1096 and was led by Peter the Hermit and the last major crusade, the Eighth, left in 1210, and was led by Saint Louis. There were also crusades in the northern regions of Europe, where crusading orders, the Sword Brothers and the Teutonic Knights, battled to capture lands from the Baltic pagans. The Crusaders wore a cross on their tunics and banners.

From a Peterborough Psalter, Brussels, Bibliothèque Royale
MS. 9961-62, East Anglian about 1300

ELEPHANT AND CASTLE

RICHARD THE LIONHEARTED

Richard I, King of England from 1189 to 1199, was a leader of the Third Crusade. King Richard was renowned for his bravery, his military tactics, and the crusading victories which he accomplished while his brother John misruled in England. After many battles, Richard established a peace with the Sultan Saladin which allowed pilgrims to visit the Holy Places. Richard was shipwrecked on his return from the Crusade and was made a prisoner. He was released after a huge ransom was paid to the Emperor Henry VI.

STROLLING MUSICIANS

From Queen Mary's Psalter, British Museum, Roy. MS. 2 B. vii about 1320

From Renaut de Montauban, Paris, Bibliothèque de l'Arsenal MS. 2990, f. 13, about 1400.

FOUR POOR KNIGHTS SEEKING ADVENTURE

KNIGHTS PLANNING HOW TO ATTACK A CASTLE

ATTACKING A CASTLE WITH CROSSBOW AND BATTLE-AXE

From the Tickhill Psalter, New York Public Library, Spencer MS. 26, f. 11v, English, early 14th century. The line in the scroll is from Chaucer, The Knightes Tale.

From a Peterborough Psalter, Brussels, Bibliothèque Royale →
MS. 9961-62, East Anglian about 1300

LADIES DEFENDING THE CASTLE OF LOVE WITH FLOWERS

AFTER THE BATTLE

From a Peterborough Psalter, Brussels, Bibliothèque
Royale MS. 9961-62, f. 74, East Anglian about 1300.

From the Manessa MS., c. 1320
Universitätsbibliothek, Heidelberg
Hiltbolt von Schwangäu

A KNIGHT AND TWO LADIES

EDWARD THE THIRD

King of England for 50 years — 1327 to 1377

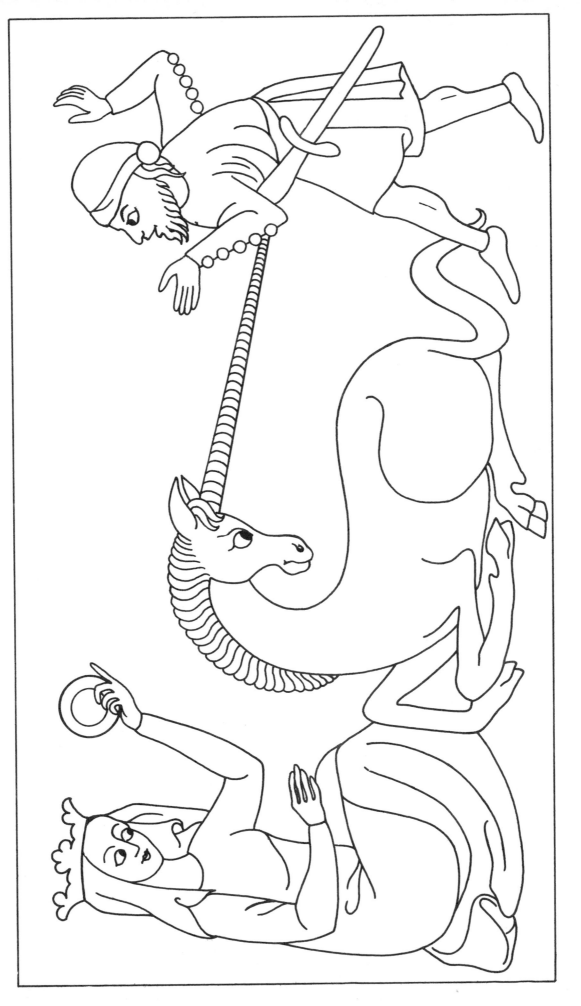

ONLY A MAIDEN COULD CATCH A UNICORN

From a monumental
brass of Sir Hugh
Hastings, c. 1347,
Elsing, Norfolk.

THE BLACK PRINCE

Edward, the Black Prince
of Wales, won the
Battle of Crécy when he
was 16 years old, but
his military adventures
caused him in time to
come to a premature
end. He was the eldest
son of King Edward the
Third and the father of
King Richard the Second.

From the Hours of Marguerite de Beaujeu,
Franco-Flemish, after 1318.
British Museum Add. MS. 36684, f. 33v

THE PLOWMAN

GEOFFREY CHAUCER

THE WIFE OF BATH

THE MILLER AND HIS WINDMILL

THE BLATANT BEAST

**SIR LANCELOT CROSSING THE SWORD BRIDGE TO
RESCUE QUEEN GUENEVERE**

**QUEEN GUENEVERE HELD CAPTIVE IN THE CASTLE OF
KING BAUDEMAGUS**

From the Psalter and Hours of Yolande, New York,
Pierpont Morgan Library MS. 729, Amiens, c. 1300

From the Manessa MS., c. 1320. Universitätsbibliothek, Heidelberg. Hartman von Aue.

A JOUST

From the Romance of Alexander,
Oxford, Bodleian Library MS. 264,
f. 92. Bruges, 1338-1344

From a German calendar, February,
Augsburg, Johann Blaubirer,
about 1485

From Marco Polo (1271-1295), Livre des Merveilles, Paris,
Bibliothèque Nationale MS. Fr. 2810, beginning of the 14th century.

**MARCO POLO SETTING OUT ON HIS JOURNEY TO THE COURT OF
KUBLAI KHAN IN CHINA**

JOAN OF ARC

Joan of Arc was tending her father's flocks when she felt an inspiration. Although she was just a young girl, she led the French to victory at Orléans and helped Charles VII to be crowned at Reims.

From Jean de Mandeville (1322-1356), Livre des Merveilles,
Paris, Bibliothèque Nationale MS. Fr. 2810, beginning of the
14th century.

NAVIGATORS AT SEA WITH AN ASTROLABE

The astrolabe was invented by the ancient Greeks to measure the altitude of heavenly
bodies. After 1480 sailors learned how to use the astrolabe to find their latitude.

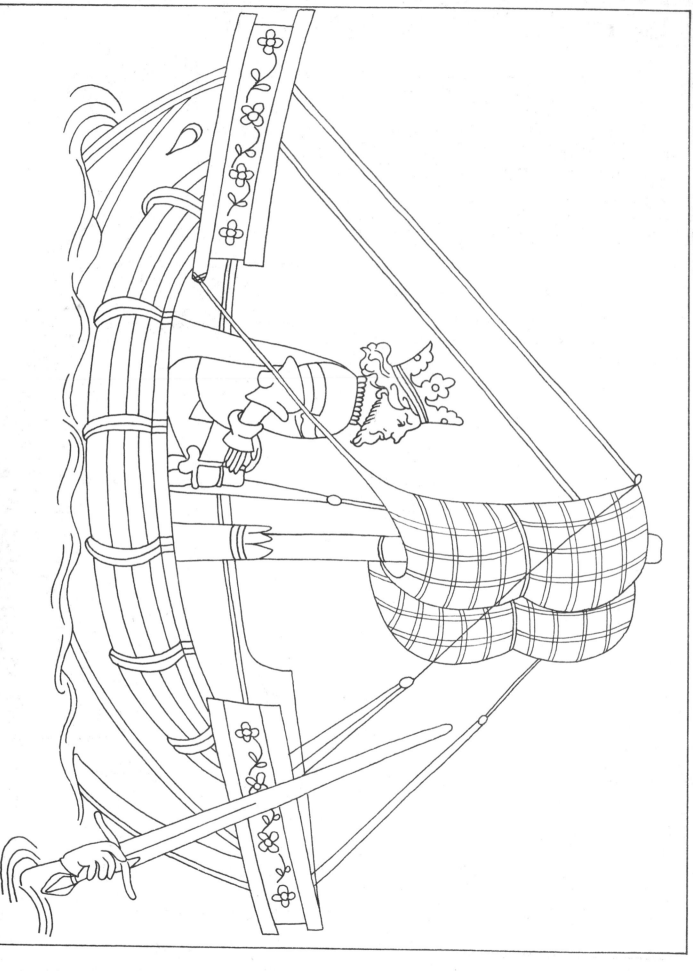

THE PASSING OF ARTHUR TO AVALON, OR GLASTONBURY, TO HEAL HIS GRIEVOUS WOUNDS, AS HIS SWORD EXCALIBUR DISAPPEARS INTO THE WATER.

From an Italian prose romance of the Round Table, North Italian, 1446, Biblioteca Nazionale, Florence, Cod. Pal. 556